D1523012

EYEWITNESS TO THE
BOMBING OF
PEARL HARBOR

BY JILL ROESLER

Published by The Child's World®
1980 Lookout Drive • Mankato, MN 56003-1705
800-599-READ • www.childsworld.com

Acknowledgments
The Child's World®: Mary Berendes, Publishing Director
Red Line Editorial: Design, editorial direction, and production
Photographs ©: Everett Historical/Shutterstock Images, cover, 1, 8, 17, 22; Ivan
Cholakov/Shutterstock Images, 4; Mary Naiden/AP Images, 7; Corbis, 10; AP
Images, 11, 18, 25; Farm Security Administration/Office of War Information/Library
of Congress, 13; Bettmann/Corbis, 14, 20, 26; David J. & Janice L. Frent Collection/
Corbis, 29

ISBN 9781634074148

LCCN 2015946225

Printed in the United States of America
Mankato, MN
December, 2015
PA02281

ABOUT THE AUTHOR

Jill Roesler is from southern Minnesota. In addition to writing children's
books, she writes for several newspapers. Her favorite subject to research
and write about is history. In her free time, Roesler enjoys reading, traveling,
and gardening.

TABLE OF CONTENTS

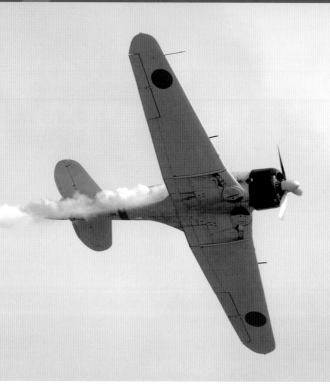

Chapter 1

SURPRISE ATTACK

December 7, 1941, was a sunny Sunday morning in Honolulu, Hawaii. Some families sat around their kitchen tables eating breakfast. Others shuffled out the door on their way to church. The sky was partly cloudy. Fighter planes and **torpedo** bombers were soaring over the city.

Residents were used to seeing fighter planes. Pearl Harbor was a naval base west of Honolulu.

The base had many U.S. Navy ships and aircraft. They were known as the Pacific Fleet. But something was different about the fighter planes that morning. The shimmering aircraft flew straight toward the harbor. That was when Daniel Inouye, a 17-year-old watching from below, noticed something strange. There were bright red circles on the wings of the planes.

The red circles showed that the planes were from Japan. "I knew what was happening," Inouye said. "And I thought my world had just come to an end."[1] The Japanese planes were attacking the Pacific Fleet.

At the time, many countries around the world were at war. Germany, Italy, and Japan were **allies** called the Axis Powers.

"I looked towards Pearl Harbor and there were puffs, dark puffs of anti-aircraft fire and then suddenly overhead three aircraft flew. They were gray in color with red dots—the Japanese symbol—and I knew that it was no play, it was real."

—*Daniel Inouye, who was 17 years old when Pearl Harbor was attacked. Inouye later became a U.S. senator.*[2]

During the 1930s, these nations tried to take control of more land. Some leaders of other nations, including Britain and France, believed that the Axis Powers were becoming too powerful. They formed their own alliance, called the Allied Powers. When Germany invaded Poland in 1939, Britain and France declared war on Germany. Soon, other countries also entered the conflict. World War II had begun.

Many Americans also thought the Axis Powers were becoming too powerful. But they did not want to go to war. President Franklin Roosevelt approved a plan to stop supplying Japan with military equipment. He also put an **embargo** on airplane fuel to Japan. Ambassador Joseph C. Grew knew that the embargo would anger Japanese leaders. He warned the president that it could lead to an attack. "War with the United States may come with dramatic and dangerous suddenness," Grew said.[3]

Roosevelt also moved the navy's Pacific Fleet from California to Pearl Harbor. The change put U.S. battleships closer to Japan and its territories. Some Japanese leaders believed that moving the ships was an unfriendly action. They thought that war with the United States would happen sooner or later. The United States had more military resources than Japan. But a sudden attack could catch American forces off-guard.

▲ People near Pearl Harbor hurried away from bomb smoke.

On the morning of December 7, 1941, Captain Logan C. Ramsey had just arrived at the Pearl Harbor Command Center. Suddenly, he spotted something unusual. "I saw . . . a single plane making a dive on Ford Island," Ramsey said.[4] Ford Island is in the center of Pearl Harbor. At first, he thought that a young pilot was acting daring. Ramsey looked for the plane's identification number. He wanted to report the pilot's behavior. But then a bomb **detonated** on the ground beneath the plane's flight path. Ramsey realized that the base was under attack.

Ramsey dashed to the radio room to alert others. He ordered the control operators to send a message on all radio frequencies. The message said, "**AIR RAID**, PEARL HARBOR. THIS IS NO DRILL."[5]

Chapter 2

THE JAPANESE PLAN

The mastermind of the air raid was Isoroku Yamamoto, the commander-in-chief of the Japanese navy fleet. Yamamoto had graduated from Harvard University. He had spent years living in the United States. He knew that Americans showed a lot of spirit during troubling times. The U.S. military would fight for its lost sailors, soldiers, and **civilians**. Yamamoto believed that only a surprise attack could hurt the United States.

Yamamoto planned for the attack to begin early in the morning. The Imperial Japanese Navy planes would reach a meeting point in the Pacific Ocean. Then the planes would attack Pearl Harbor in two **waves**. When the pilots neared Hawaii, they waited for instructions. Commander Mitsuo Fuchida was leading the attack.

An experienced pilot, Fuchida watched for the right moment to begin. Sitting in his fighter jet, he peered through his binoculars at the ships in Pearl Harbor. The sky was clear, except for a light morning mist. At 6:10 a.m., Fuchida sent a radio message instructing the pilots to take off toward Hawaii. Nearly two hundred torpedo bombers, dive bombers, and fighter planes sped toward the harbor. In less than two hours, they would reach the base.

As the planes headed for the harbor, Fuchida looked for the ships and **aircraft carriers**. All eight battleships were in place. But he did not see any aircraft carriers. The seven U.S. aircraft carriers were out at sea when the Japanese navy arrived. Fuchida

▲ Commander Mitsuo Fuchida led the Pearl Harbor attack.

had hoped to destroy the carriers. That way, the U.S. Navy forces could not defend themselves.

When the planes reached the harbor at 7:49 a.m., Commander Fuchida gave the signal to start the attack. Bomber planes launched their torpedoes. By 7:53 a.m., they had hit their first

◀ Isoroku Yamamoto planned the Japanese attack on Pearl Harbor.

targets. Japanese naval leaders radioed a message to their homeland: "Tora . . . Tora . . . Tora." These code words meant that the surprise attack was successful.

The first bomb fell on Wheeler Field, an Army Air Force field north of the harbor. Japanese leaders wanted to prevent U.S. pilots from launching a return attack. After that, Japanese forces would work their way toward Battleship Row. Meanwhile, U.S. military officers were just waking up to the attack.

Bombs hit Hickam Field, an Army Air Force base near ▶ Pearl Harbor.

Chapter 3

RESPONDING TO THE ATTACK

U.S. Second Lieutenant Francis Gabreski was lying in bed in the officers' quarters near Wheeler Field. Suddenly, he heard a shrill noise. Gabreski had been out late at a dance the night before. When he heard the noise, he was confused. "At first I thought it was one of the Navy patrol planes," he remembered. Navy planes often flew

◄ Second Lieutenant Francis Gabreski and other pilots saved planes at Wheeler Field.

in the area. "But then there was another hit, this time pretty close. I heard an airplane flying over the rooftops so I ran out to look. I just barely caught a glimpse of a big red circle on the plane. The rear gunner was spraying the buildings with bullets."[6] Gabreski ran inside. He began to warn the rest of the pilots.

"It dawned on me . . . that this was an actual bombing," Gabreski said. "Our airplane **hangars** were being hit."[7] He and the other officers rushed to save the planes.

At Wheeler Field, U.S. warplanes were parked wingtip to wingtip. They were easy targets for an attack. The Japanese forces began to bomb the warplanes. U.S. Navy men rushed

"I got out of my bed and looked out the window and saw a plume of smoke in Pearl Harbor. . . . I got up and hurried downstairs and outside. The sun was shining. I looked around and saw this airplane with a red circle on its side. It was a fighter plane flying low toward the airfield—so low I could see the pilot. I can still see him today."

—*Staff Sergeant Bob Kroner, Army Signal Corps*[8]

outside to stop them. Some were still in their pajamas. At the time, Wheeler Field held approximately 90 planes. Gabreski and the others worked together to move planes out of the way. They managed to save about 30 planes.

Suddenly, an ear-splitting noise rang through the naval station. A plane had just dropped a bomb on the USS *Arizona*. This U.S. battleship was carrying more than one million pounds of gunpowder when it was hit. When the bomb hit the ship, the gunpowder helped cause a massive explosion.

A fighter plane dropped a bomb on the USS *Arizona*, ▶ causing a deadly explosion.

Chapter 4

BOMBS ON THE BATTLESHIPS

The explosion on the *Arizona* sent a giant fireball into the sky. The ship quickly began to sink. Only nine minutes after the explosion, the ship hit the bottom of the harbor. The explosion and sinking killed 1,177 crew members onboard.

◀ While sailors attempted to save planes, a bomb exploded on the USS *Shaw*.

One sailor watched the destruction from another battleship, the USS *Nevada*. He saw the *Arizona* "jump at least 15 or 20 feet upward in the water and sort of break in two."[9] An hour later, the *Nevada* was hit with five bombs. Although the battleship was greatly damaged, sailors managed to shoot down three Japanese planes.

Meanwhile, the second wave of Japanese fighter planes headed for the harbor. They arrived at the base at 8:54 a.m. This second group included 167 bombers and fighter planes. This time, the Japanese forces hit the USS *Pennsylvania*. They also hit an oil tank between two destroyer ships, the USS *Cassin* and the USS *Downes*. The explosion set the *Cassin* in motion. It crashed into the *Downes*. A half-hour later, another bomb exploded on the USS *Shaw*.

Doris Miller was a mess cook on the *Shaw*. He had joined the navy to explore the world. Miller was doing laundry when the attack on Pearl Harbor began. After the bomb exploded, he reported to the deck of the ship. He rushed to bring wounded sailors to safety. The ship had two massive machine guns. But many sailors were too injured to fire them. An officer ordered Miller to help load one of the guns.

▲ Doris Miller received a Navy Cross for his bravery at Pearl Harbor.

Miller had never used a machine gun before. He had no weapons training. But for the next 15 minutes, he loaded the gun and fired it at planes. He kept firing until it ran out of ammunition.

Miller later received a Navy Cross for his courage. He was the first black person to receive this honor.

In all, American navy men shot down 15 Japanese planes. But the attack had been successful. The United States had suffered many losses. Nineteen U.S. ships, including eight battleships, were damaged or destroyed. At 9:45 a.m., the Japanese navy planes began to leave the harbor. Many of the pilots were excited by the success of the attack. They wanted to return for a third wave. But Commander Fuchida insisted that two waves were enough. He did not know where the U.S. aircraft carriers were. If they returned, the United States could launch a counterattack.

"It wasn't hard. I just pulled the trigger and [the machine gun] worked fine. I had watched the others with these guns. I guess I fired her for about fifteen minutes. I think I got one of those Japanese planes. They were diving pretty close to us."

—Doris Miller[10]

Chapter 5

AFTER THE ATTACK

The attack was over, but more challenges lay ahead. Medics set up temporary hospitals in schools near Pearl Harbor. Sailors carried their wounded comrades to these areas. Nurses and doctors worked for long hours to help them. Many of the sailors' injuries were too severe to be treated. The attack left 2,390 people dead and 1,178 wounded. At night, hospitals turned down lights to prevent another attack. Nurses worked in near darkness.

Robert Hardaway III was a doctor at a local hospital. "Just as I was going into the hospital, an ambulance came roaring in," he said. "I ran over and opened the back door and there were four soldiers in there. One was already dead and I knew then that this was a war."[11] As Hardaway tended to wounded patients, a local radio station played "The Star-Spangled Banner." Years later, he remembered hearing the words "the bombs bursting in air, gave proof through the night that our flag was still there."

Meanwhile, reports of the attack were reaching the U.S. mainland. One report came from a radio station in Pittsburgh,

"I was assigned to cover the emergency room of the hospital. The first victims of the Japanese-American war were brought there on that bright Sunday morning. Bombs were still dropping over the city as ambulances screamed off into the heart of destruction."

—*Betty McIntosh, a reporter for the* Honolulu Star-Bulletin[12]

Pennsylvania. "We have witnessed this morning the attack of Pearl Harbor and a severe bombing of Pearl Harbor by army planes," the reporter announced. "It's no joke. It's a real war."[13]

As Americans learned of the attack, hundreds of people worked to clean up the destroyed harbor. *New York Times* reporter Robert Trumbull was in Honolulu. He described sailors caring for a damaged battleship "as a mother would tend a sick child."[14] Cleaning and repairs took years. Some ships, including the *Arizona*, were destroyed. But sailors were able to repair most of the damaged ships.

Hawaiians sorted through wreckage in the days after ▶ the attack.

Chapter 6

WAR

As Americans worked to rebuild Pearl Harbor, the Imperial Japanese Navy celebrated victory. Yet some people were nervous about the results of the attack. Isoroku Yamamoto warned that the United States would seek revenge.

"You men trained hard and patiently," Yamamoto said. "Your operation against Pearl Harbor was a great success. You must remember, however, that . . . we have only entered upon the first stage of this war. . . . There are many more battles ahead."[15] Yamamoto knew that the Americans would join together to fight.

Yamamoto's prediction was correct. The day after the attack, President Roosevelt addressed Americans in a radio speech. Roosevelt described the attack as shameful. Japanese forces had attacked the United States without declaring war first. The president called December 7, 1941, "a date that will live in **infamy**."[16] He also expressed pride in the American military. Roosevelt said that Americans would come together to fight.

Roosevelt asked Congress to declare war on Japan. The Senate and the House of Representatives took a vote. Only one

"I think all the people of the United States should be behind the president because his speech was an excellent performance of his duty towards the people. . . . And I assure you that every working man will be behind the president in his hour of need."

—*Richard Kwan of New York City in a "Man on the Street" interview, December 8, 1941*[17]

person voted against declaring war. At 4:10 p.m. on December 8, 1941, Roosevelt signed the declaration. He wore a black armband to remember victims of the Pearl Harbor attack. The United States had entered World War II. A few days later, the United States declared war on Germany and Italy, too.

Hundreds of Americans sent messages to the White House. Most supported the decision to go to war. One person wrote that Roosevelt's "courage pulled us together."[18] People bought pins that said "Remember Pearl Harbor." Thousands of young men volunteered for military service. It was the start of a long conflict. For the next four years, the United States was at war.

Some Americans used pins to honor those who died ▶ at Pearl Harbor.

GLOSSARY

aircraft carriers (AIR-kraft KAIR-ee-yurz): Aircraft carriers are warships that can hold and move planes. At Pearl Harbor, Japanese leaders looked for U.S. aircraft carriers.

air raid (AIR RAID): In an air raid, attackers drop bombs from airplanes. Japanese forces began an air raid on Pearl Harbor.

allies (AL-eyes): Allies are countries that join together to help one another. During World War II, Japan, Germany, and Italy were allies.

civilians (si-VIL-yunz): Civilians are people who are not in the military. Some civilians were injured during the attack.

detonated (DET-un-ayt-ed): When something is detonated, it explodes. Japanese pilots dropped bombs that detonated on Pearl Harbor.

embargo (em-BAR-go): An embargo is an official ban on trade. In 1941, the United States had an embargo on the oil trade with Japan.

hangars (HANG-arz): Hangars are buildings that store aircraft. At Pearl Harbor, Japanese pilots targeted airplane hangars.

infamy (IN-fuh-mee): Events or people with infamy are famous for bad reasons. President Roosevelt said that the date of December 7, 1941, would "live in infamy."

torpedo (tor-PEE-doh): A torpedo is a weapon that explodes on a ship or other vessel. A plane dropped a torpedo on a battleship.

waves (WAYVZ): Waves are groups of vehicles or soldiers that land or attack at a certain time. Two waves of Japanese warplanes attacked Pearl Harbor.

SOURCE NOTES

1. "Civil Rights – Japanese Americans." *The War: At Home*. PBS, 2007. Web. 26 May 2015.

2. "Sen. Daniel Inouye on Pearl Harbor, after 70 Years." *Tell Me More*. NPR, 7 December 2011. Web. 26 May 2015.

3. Evan Mawdsley. *December 1941: Twelve Days that Began a World War*. New Haven, CT: Yale University Press, 2011. Print. 74.

4-5. Logan C. Ramsey. *Air Raid, Pearl Harbor. This Is No Drill*. Annapolis, MD: Naval Institute Press, 1981. Print. 35.

6-7. "World War II: The Attack on Pearl Harbor." *Hawaii Aviation*. The State of Hawaii Department of Transportation, Airports Division, n.d. Web. 26 May 2015.

8. David Venditta. "93-Year-Old Pearl Harbor Survivor Remembers Pearl Harbor Attack." *The Morning Call*. Tribune Publishing, 7 December 2012. Web. 10 August 2015.

9. "Pearl Harbor Time Line." *Remembering Pearl Harbor History*. National Geographic, n.d. Web. 26 May 2015.

10. Gaius Chamberlain. "Doris Miller." *Great Black Heroes*. Adscape International, LLC, 25 January 2012. Web. 26 May 2015.

11. Chelsea Davis. "Pearl Harbor Army medic recalls tragic day." *Connect*. Hawaii News Now, 8 December 2014. Web. 26 May 2015.

12. Elizabeth P. McIntosh. "Honolulu after Pearl Harbor: A report published for the first time, 71 years later." *The Washington Post*. The Washington Post, 6 December 2012. Web. 26 May 2015.

13. "Bulletin from Honolulu." *Heard over WCAE (Pittsburgh, PA)*. UMKC University Libraries, 10 September 2008 and 7 December 1941. Web. 26 May 2015.

14. Robert Trumbull. "Pearl Harbor: One Day of Infamy, Two Years of Hard Work." *The New York Times*. The New York Times Company, 7 December 2006. Web. 26 May 2015.

15. Gordon William Prange. *At Dawn We Slept: The Untold Story of Pearl Harbor*. New York: Penguin, 2001. Print. 578.

16. Robert J. Brown. *Manipulating the Ether: The Power of Broadcast Radio in Thirties America*. Jefferson, NC: McFarland, 1998. Print. 117.

17. "'Man-on-the-Street,' New York, New York, December 8, 1941." *American Memory*. Library of Congress, n.d. Web. 26 May 2015.

18. Robert J. Brown. 119.

TO LEARN MORE

Books

Adams, Simon. *World War II*. New York: DK Publishing, 2014.

Demuth, Patricia Brennan. *What Was Pearl Harbor?* New York: Grosset & Dunlap, 2013.

Krieg, Katherine. *The Attack on Pearl Harbor*. Ann Arbor, MI: Cherry Lake, 2013.

Web Sites

Visit our Web site for links about the bombing of Pearl Harbor:

childsworld.com/links

Note to Parents, Teachers, and Librarians: We routinely verify our Web links to make sure they are safe and active sites. So encourage your readers to check them out!

INDEX